THE BRUMBACK LIBRARY

OF VAN WERT COUNTY

VAN WERT, OHIO

LIZARDS
AND DRAGONS

Design
David West
Children's Book Design
Illustrations
Tessa Barwick
Picture Research
Cecilia Weston-Baker
Editor
Denny Robson
Consultant
John Stidworthy

DB

© Aladdin Books Ltd

Designed and produced by
Aladdin Books Ltd
70 Old Compton Street
London W1

*First published in the
United States in 1988 by*
Gloucester Press
387 Park Avenue South
New York, NY 10016

Printed in Belgium

ISBN 0-531-17075-6

Library of Congress Catalog
Card Number: 87-82899

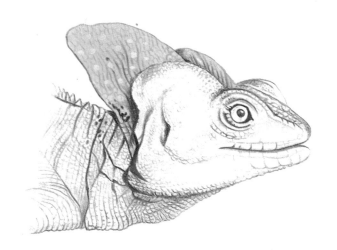

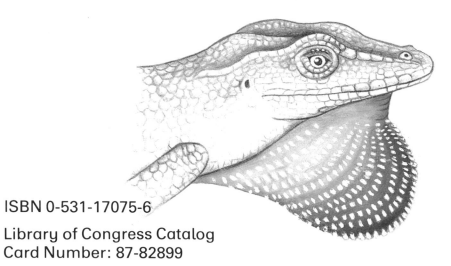

This book tells you about all the different types of lizards – where they live, what they look like and how they survive. Find out some surprising facts in the boxes on each page. The Identification Chart at the back will help you when you see lizards in the zoo.

 or

The little square shows you the size of the lizard. Each side represents 2ft (60cm).

A red square means that a lizard is in need of protection. Turn to the Survival File.

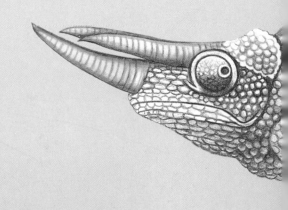

The picture opposite shows an anole lizard with a flat throat sac

FIRST SIGHT

LIZARDS
AND DRAGONS

Lionel Bender

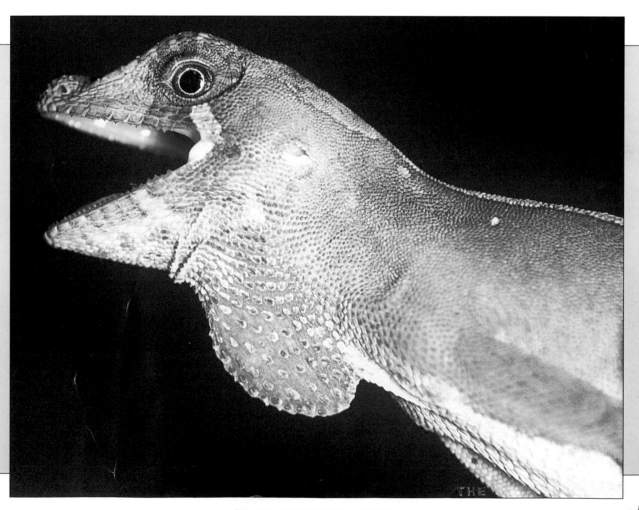

GLOUCESTER PRESS

New York · London · Toronto · Sydney

Introduction

There are about 3,750 different species of lizards in the world. This makes them one of the biggest groups of backboned animals. Lizards are found in all kinds of surroundings and in most areas, except for the polar regions and on mountaintops where it is too cold. Some 100 million years ago in the time of the dinosaurs, giant lizards called mosasaurs swam through the seas. Modern lizards stay almost entirely on land and beside fresh water.

Like other reptiles, lizards breathe air using lungs and have scaly skins. They are enormously varied. Some look very strange. Others have surprising habits or abilities. This book is an introduction to just some of these interesting reptiles.

Contents

◁ **A chameleon feeds on a locust**

Some lizards manage to keep their bodies as warm as ours at 98.6°F (37°C). Some desert lizards, like the Desert Iguana, can have body temperatures as high as 115°F (46°C). Lizards become sluggish at 59°-68°F (15-20°C).

midday

early morning

late afternoon

Lizards warm up by basking in the morning sun

They hide in the shade when the sun is hottest

They bask again as the day grows cooler

Warming to the task

Lizards, like other reptiles, are cold-blooded. This means their bodies usually work less actively than ours and they do not produce heat. Lizards have to rely on their surroundings to keep their bodies warm enough to work properly. This is why they are most common in hot countries.

Even in very hot places, lizards keep their bodies at a constant temperature. They move to avoid getting too hot or too cold. In colder climates they hibernate during winter, going underground and becoming cold and inactive.

Eggs and babies

Most lizards lay eggs, which usually have a leathery shell. They may dig holes to act as nests or use ready-made hiding places. Tropical monitor lizards may lay as many as 60 eggs. Some geckos only lay one or two. The typical number is about 10 eggs.

Only a few kinds of lizards actually guard the eggs. They may take two weeks to hatch or as long as three months, depending on the warmth of the surroundings. In lizards like the European Common Lizard and some skinks the eggs are not laid at all. They are kept inside the mother's body until hatching. Baby lizards are smaller versions of their parents and can look after themselves as soon as they are born.

A baby gecko lizard hatches from a clutch of eggs

Giants and pygmies

Lizards vary enormously in size. Most are quite small animals, ranging from about 6in to 12in (15cm to 30cm) long, which includes a tail about as long as the body. Some lizards are very tiny, like the delicate transparent geckos which are only 2in (5cm) long.

At the other end of the scale the big monitor lizards from tropical Africa, Asia and Australia are the giants among the lizards. Several species grow to 7ft (2m) or more. They are such fierce hunters that the biggest of all is known as the Komodo Dragon. Other "dragons" include the Water Dragon of Australia and the Sailed Dragon of the East Indies. Some iguanas and tegu lizards of South America are also very large.

The gecko Sphaerodactylus macrolepsis could fit on a matchbook

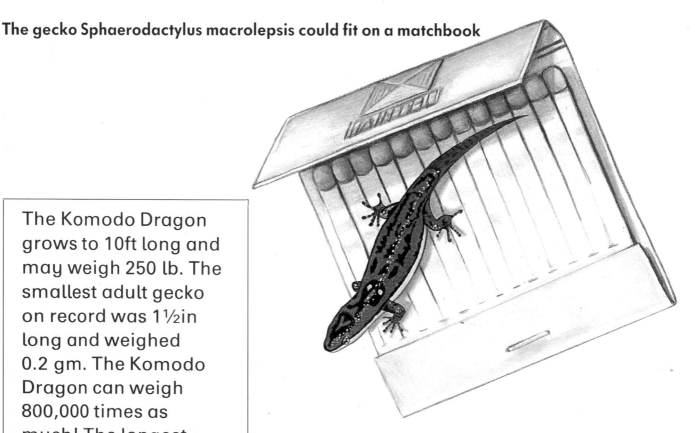

The Komodo Dragon grows to 10ft long and may weigh 250 lb. The smallest adult gecko on record was 1½in long and weighed 0.2 gm. The Komodo Dragon can weigh 800,000 times as much! The longest lizard is Salvador's Monitor at 13ft long.

The meat-eating Komodo Dragon lives on just a few Indonesian islands ▷

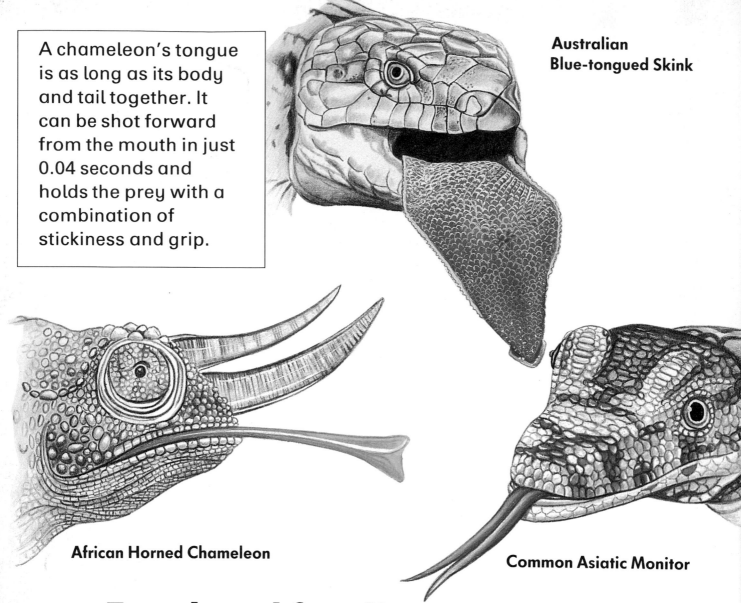

A chameleon's tongue is as long as its body and tail together. It can be shot forward from the mouth in just 0.04 seconds and holds the prey with a combination of stickiness and grip.

Australian Blue-tongued Skink

African Horned Chameleon

Common Asiatic Monitor

Food and feeding

Lizards nearly all feed on other animals. The Komodo Dragon can kill and eat a small deer. Some of the large monitor lizards eat other reptiles or mammals and birds. But for most lizards, insects are the commonest type of food. A lizard's small sharp teeth and jaws are suitable for seizing and swallowing prey rather than chewing.

A few lizards are specialist feeders. The Australian Thorny Devil, for example, feeds on ants. The diet of the North American Gila Monster includes eggs. Many of the large iguanas and some of the largest skinks have a vegetarian diet. The Galapagos Sea Iguana seems to live entirely on seaweed.

A Horned Chameleon captures a fly with its extending tongue ▷

Senses

A lizard can often see its prey or enemy long before it can hear it. Most lizards can see sharply and in color. This means that species like anoles can change their body color to signal their presence and mood to one another. Lizards have only a weak sense of hearing. Geckos have the most highly developed ears. They are the noisiest of lizards, communicating with loud clicks and barks.

A lizard can smell food or mates from many feet away using its nose. But more important to its sense of smell is Jacobson's organ in the roof of the mouth. The tongue collects particles from the air which are put in the roof of the mouth for smelling. Monitors have long, forked tongues to help in this.

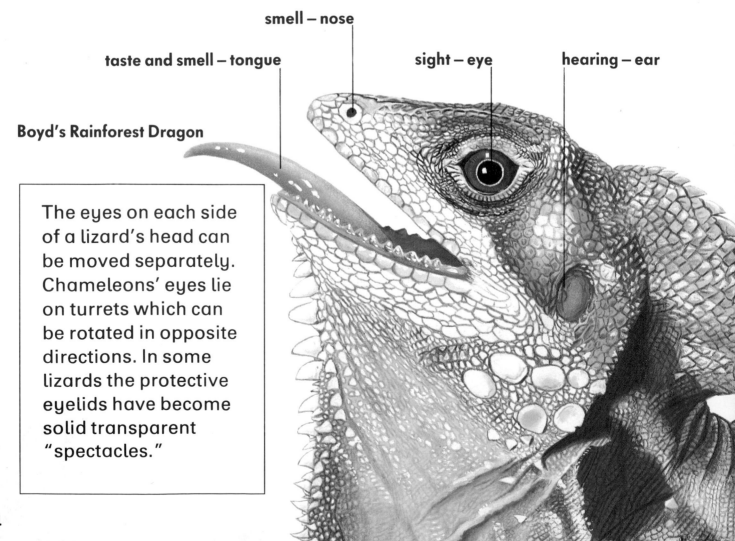

smell – nose

taste and smell – tongue

sight – eye

hearing – ear

Boyd's Rainforest Dragon

The eyes on each side of a lizard's head can be moved separately. Chameleons' eyes lie on turrets which can be rotated in opposite directions. In some lizards the protective eyelids have become solid transparent "spectacles."

Courtship

Many male lizards use colors and special behavior to attract females for mating. The male African Rainbow Agama, for example, has an orange head, blue back, and an orange and black tail that make him obvious. When a possible mate appears, he makes a series of slow push-ups to attract attention. Similar displays are used to warn off rivals, except that the push-ups are faster and the throat is expanded.

Male and female lizards often look very different. This makes it easy for the sexes to recognize one another. Usually males are more colorful. They may also have horns, as in some African chameleons, or crests, as in the South American Basilisk.

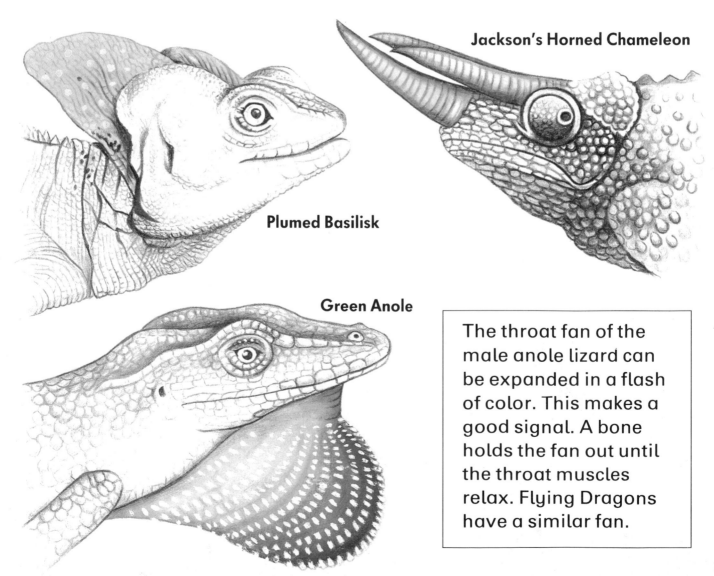

Jackson's Horned Chameleon

Plumed Basilisk

Green Anole

The throat fan of the male anole lizard can be expanded in a flash of color. This makes a good signal. A bone holds the fan out until the throat muscles relax. Flying Dragons have a similar fan.

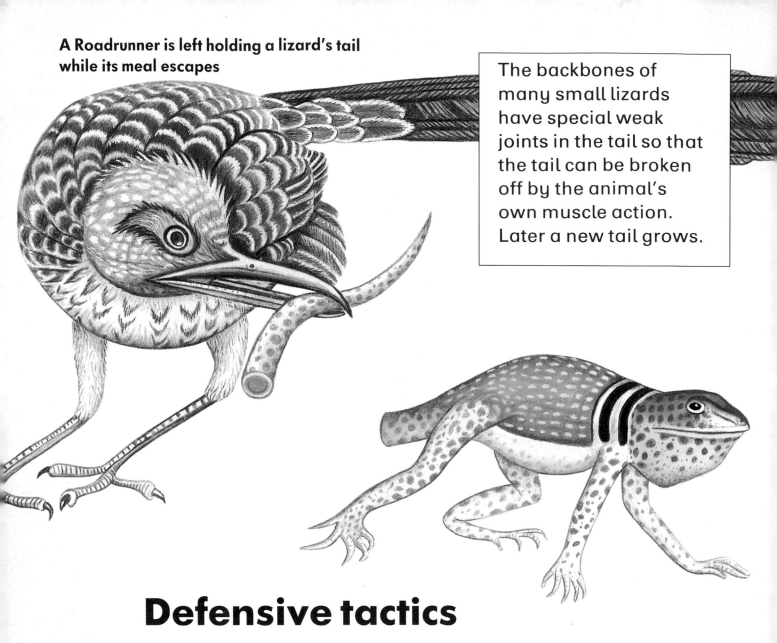

A Roadrunner is left holding a lizard's tail while its meal escapes

The backbones of many small lizards have special weak joints in the tail so that the tail can be broken off by the animal's own muscle action. Later a new tail grows.

Defensive tactics

Lizards have many enemies, like hawks and cats, which would eat them if given the chance. They protect themselves in several ways. Many, like the chameleons, depend on camouflage where their body color matches the background. Some geckos and Side-blotched Lizards have stripes or blotches which break up their outline. Lizards also keep still for long periods which makes them difficult to see.

The Bearded and Frilled lizards of Australia warn off enemies by looking bigger than they really are. Geckos shed their tail to confuse attackers while they escape. Some skinks shed patches of skin to confuse predators, and the Horned Lizard of North America squirts blood from its eyes when attacked.

The Australian Frilled Lizard expands it neck frill when alarmed ▷

Spines and armor

Spines and armor give lizards protection from both enemies and injury. African plated lizards have a series of flat plates of bone in ther scales which form a complete suit of bony armor. The European Slow-worm also has protective bony plates in the skin.

Other lizards have long spiny scales. Their prickly bodies make them difficult to attack or swallow. Spiny scales are particularly common in some of the desert lizards. Probably the spiniest of all are the horned toads of North America and the Thorny Devil of Australia. Among African girdled lizards, many species swing their spiny tails as clubs in defense.

The Armadillo Girdled Lizard curls up when attacked

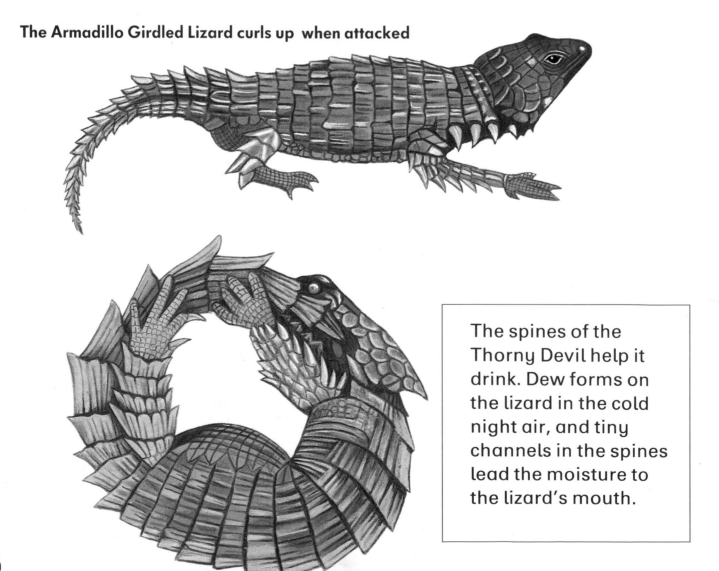

The spines of the Thorny Devil help it drink. Dew forms on the lizard in the cold night air, and tiny channels in the spines lead the moisture to the lizard's mouth.

20

Some lizards appear to fly. The Flying Dragon of the Far East has flaps of skin on its sides. These can be spread wide supported by long ribs. On these "wings" the lizard can glide as far as 65ft (20m).

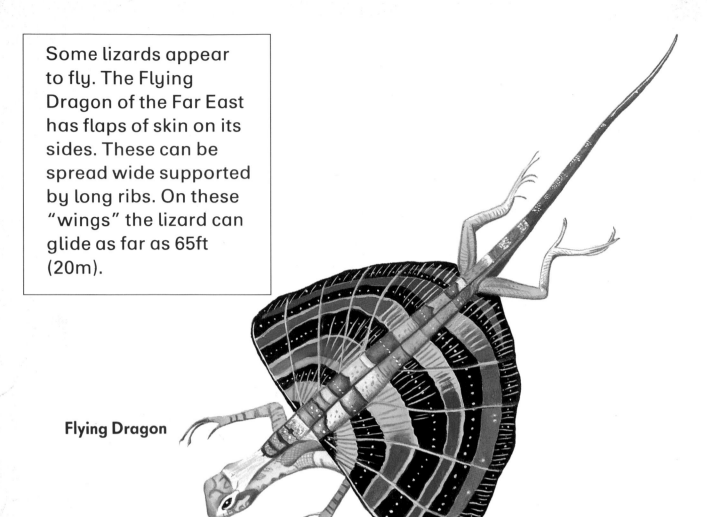

Flying Dragon

Climbing and flying

With their light bodies, sharp claws and long tails for balance, lizards are well equipped to scramble over rocks, bushes and trees. Some have become specialist climbers. Chameleons have feet that can grip, two toes going one way around a twig, the other three the other way. They also have a tail that can grip. They can turn their eyes so that both look forward, which gives them good judgment of distance.

Geckos are another family "built" for climbing. They can even walk upside-down on a ceiling. The undersides of their toes have ridges to help them cling. These ridges have tiny projections that can clasp imperfections in a surface as smooth as glass.

Ridges under a gecko's toes show clearly as it climbs a pane of glass ▷

Disappearing legs

Many groups of lizards contain members which have limbs that are reduced in size or even absent. The slow-worm family, for example, ranges from alligator lizards which have normal legs to Slow-worm and glass "snakes" which have no legs at all.

Lizards with reduced legs, like skinks and flap-footed lizards, are usually burrowers or animals that move in thick undergrowth. In these places it is easier to move along by bending the body than by using legs. Legless lizards have longer bodies and more ribs and bones in the backbone than their legged relatives. Their ear openings are often smaller or absent and their eyes may be small and ineffective.

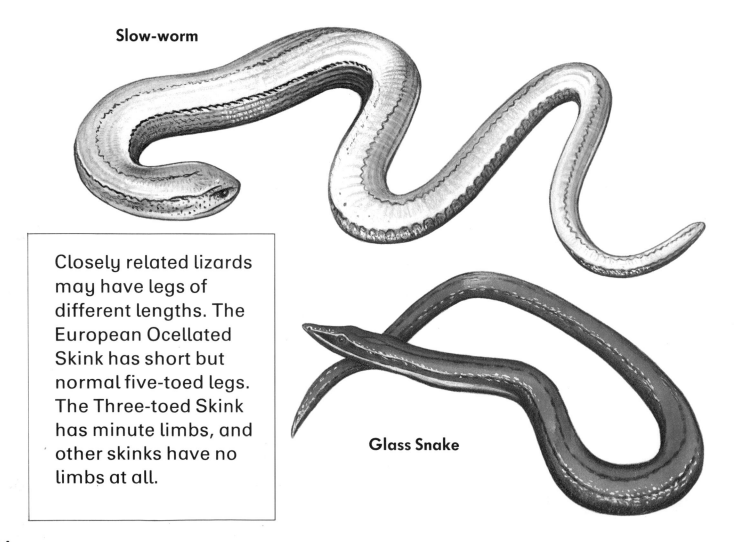

Slow-worm

Glass Snake

Closely related lizards may have legs of different lengths. The European Ocellated Skink has short but normal five-toed legs. The Three-toed Skink has minute limbs, and other skinks have no limbs at all.

The Gila Monster of the North American deserts is a lizard with a venomous bite. Its venom is very effective in subduing bird and mammal prey. It stores fat in its tail and can go for months without food.

Gila Monster

Stump-tailed Skink

Desert dwellers

Lizards are well adapted to living in dry areas. They are good at keeping water in their bodies. A lizard's skin is dry and scaly and water is lost through it very slowly. Lizards can produce urine as a semi-solid paste. Desert lizards may avoid daytime heat by burrowing, or if they stay active, by raising their bodies away from the hot sand.

Because their bodies work slowly, lizards burn up food slowly. They are able to survive periods without food better than many other animals. This is useful in areas where food is scarce. Desert dwellers like the Australian Stump-tailed Skink can store fat in their tails and use it up when food cannot be found.

A Frilled Lizard runs on its back legs keeping its body away from the hot sand ▷

Survival file

Lizards have lived on Earth for many millions of years. Today they are under threat more than at any time in the past. The greatest danger comes from growing numbers of people. As our population increases, more towns and farms are created. They change and pollute the countryside so much that it can become difficult for lizards to survive.

The Galapagos Land Iguana suffers from human activity

Large iguanas and monitor lizards are eaten by humans in tropical parts of the world. Monitors are also illegally hunted to make lizard-skin pocketbooks. But the lizards most in danger are those whose habitat has been disturbed. Also in danger are lizards which live in such small numbers or in such a small area that they could be wiped out easily.

Many kinds of lizard live only on one island, group of islands or on one range of mountains. An example is the Komodo Dragon from Komodo Island and nearby areas. Such lizards are completely adapted to their particular home. Any changes could be fatal.

A Lace Monitor in a zoo

The Galapagos Land Iguana has suffered from human activity. Islanders let goats go wild which now compete with the iguanas for food plants. The iguanas have disappeared from some of the islands but every effort is being made to preserve those that remain. In Great Britain the Sand Lizard has become rare mainly because houses and roads are being built on the land where it lives.

Some reptiles can be helped by breeding them in captivity, but many are difficult to keep. Either the adults fail to breed or the young die soon after hatching. We need to learn more about their lives in the wild and about their needs for heat, sunlight and food.

The Sand Lizard is disappearing in Britain

Identification chart

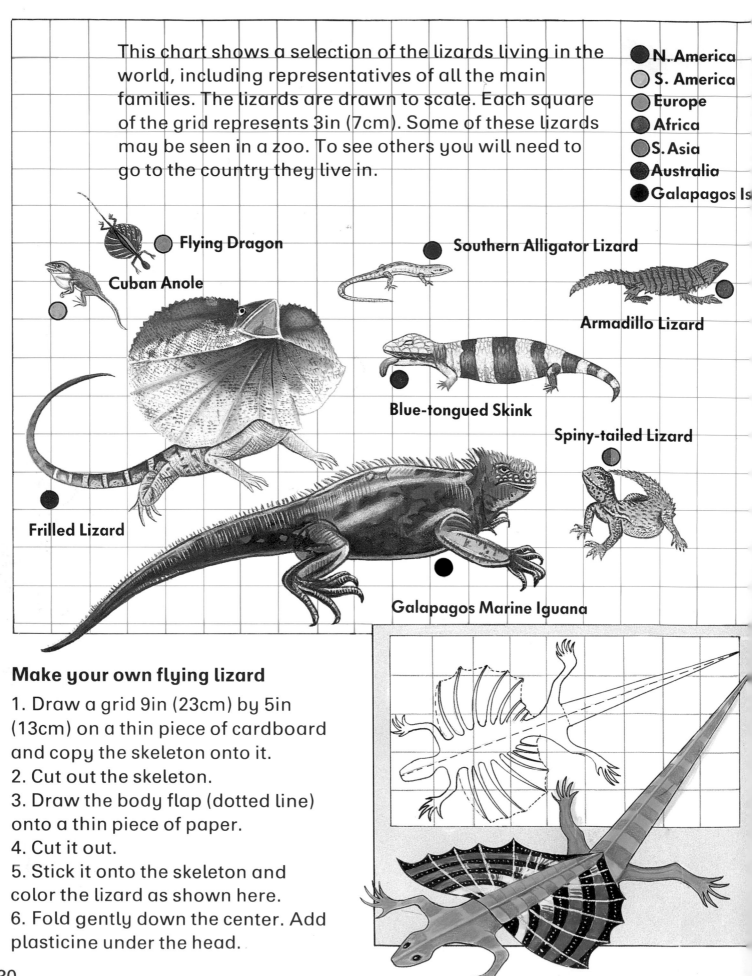

This chart shows a selection of the lizards living in the world, including representatives of all the main families. The lizards are drawn to scale. Each square of the grid represents 3in (7cm). Some of these lizards may be seen in a zoo. To see others you will need to go to the country they live in.

- N. America
- S. America
- Europe
- Africa
- S. Asia
- Australia
- Galapagos Is

Flying Dragon

Cuban Anole

Southern Alligator Lizard

Armadillo Lizard

Blue-tongued Skink

Spiny-tailed Lizard

Frilled Lizard

Galapagos Marine Iguana

Make your own flying lizard

1. Draw a grid 9in (23cm) by 5in (13cm) on a thin piece of cardboard and copy the skeleton onto it.
2. Cut out the skeleton.
3. Draw the body flap (dotted line) onto a thin piece of paper.
4. Cut it out.
5. Stick it onto the skeleton and color the lizard as shown here.
6. Fold gently down the center. Add plasticine under the head.

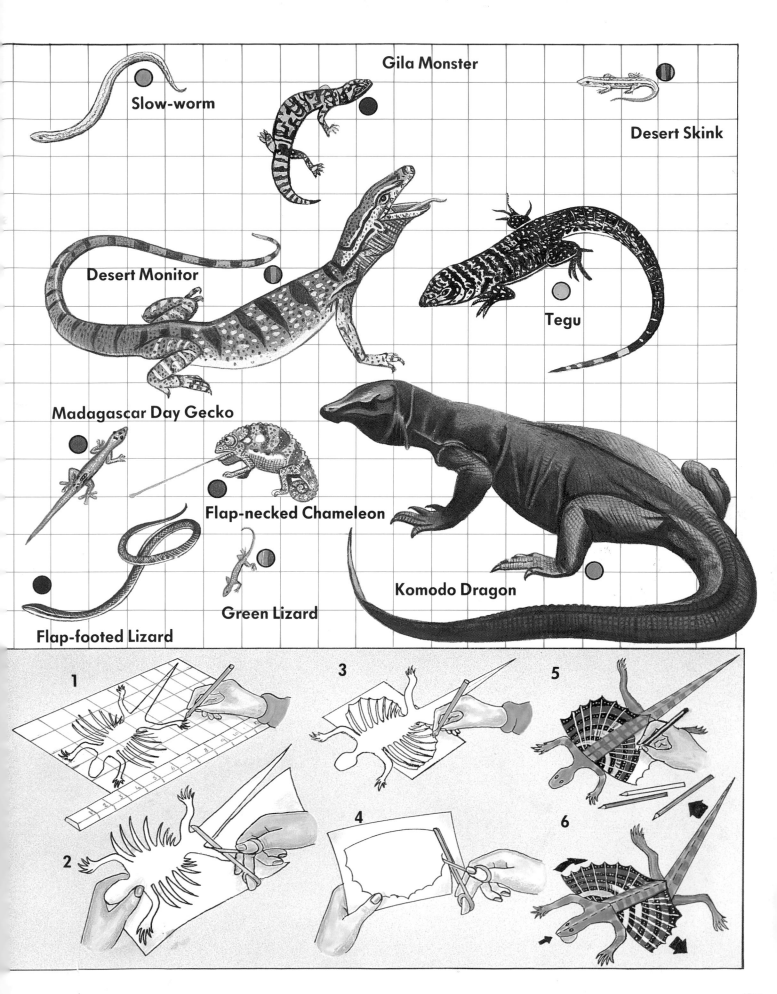

Slow-worm

Gila Monster

Desert Skink

Desert Monitor

Tegu

Madagascar Day Gecko

Flap-necked Chameleon

Komodo Dragon

Flap-footed Lizard

Green Lizard

1

2

3

4

5

6

Index

Photographic Credits:
Cover and pages 9, 23 and 29 (top); Planet Earth; title page and pages 7 and 19: Ardea; intro and pages 8 and 29: Survival Anglia; pages 11, 13, 15, 16, 21 and 29 (bottom): Bruce Colman; page 25: Nature Photographers; page 27: NHPA.

PRINTED IN BELGIUM BY
proost
INTERNATIONAL BOOK PRODUCTION